Contents

QUEEN VICTORIA AND THE VICTORIANS

Queen Victoria became queen in 1837 and ruled for sixty-three years. During her long reign, life changed for everyone – especially children.

The Victorians

The people who lived in Britain at this time are called the Victorians. The number of Victorians almost doubled during Queen Victoria's reign, mostly because people began to live for longer. People often had large families, with six or more children. Sadly, children often died in childhood.

Queen Victoria and her husband, Prince Albert, had nine children of their own. Family life was important to the royal couple.

A changing world

A huge number of families moved from villages to find work in towns and cities. Millions of houses were built for them to live in. Children born into poor homes had very different lives from those born into wealthier homes. This continued throughout the Victorian period. However, many changes, including free schooling and laws about working hours and conditions, improved the chances in life for most children.

By the end of the Victorian period, older children were still working in mills, but they were half-timers, splitting their day between work and school.

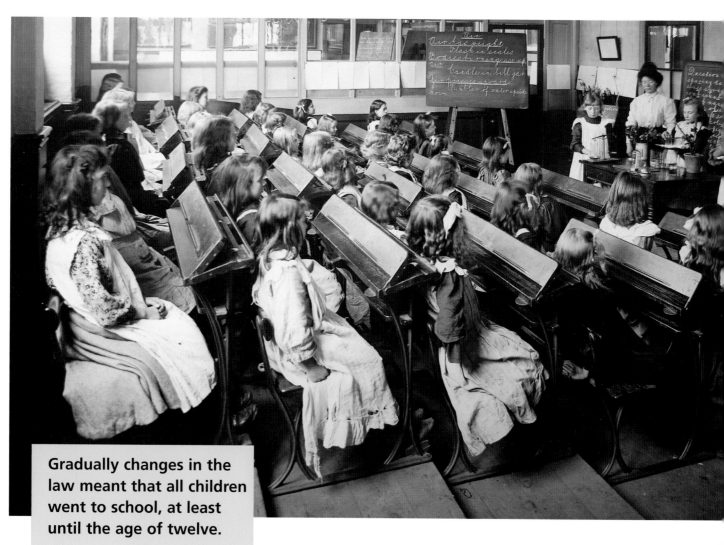

Gradually changes in the law meant that all children went to school, at least until the age of twelve.

THE MOVE TO TOWNS

In early Victorian times, nearly three-quarters of the British people lived in villages. By 1901, three-quarters of them lived in towns and cities, many of them crammed into newly-built houses.

Homes for workers

Life in the country was hard for poor people. Thousands of farm workers moved to industrial cities, such as Leeds, Birmingham, Liverpool, Nottingham and Manchester, seeking better-paid work in new factories. Streets of houses were built for workers to rent, often in the town centre near the factories and workshops.

Many houses were built joined together in rows, known as terraces. Two families lived in each of these houses – one upstairs and the other downstairs.

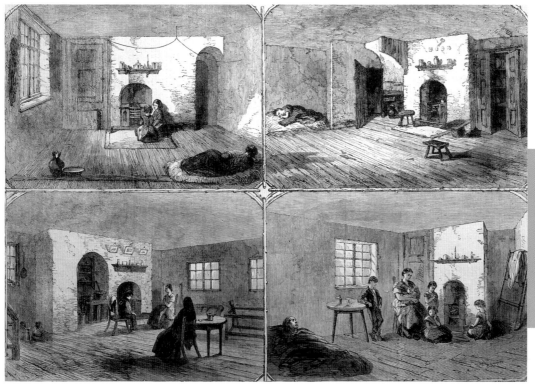

Poor families could not afford much furniture. Often, two or three children shared a bed.

Privies had a bucket, which night-soil men came to empty once a week.

Back-to-back houses

Builders crammed in as many homes as they could into city centres. They built houses back-to-back or in a court. Courts were reached from the street through a narrow passageway. These houses had no running water. Families fetched buckets of water from a standpipe or a nearby pump and shared an outside lavatory, known as a privy. Some courts also shared a wash-house for laundry.

Notice how narrow the space is between the two rows of houses in this court.

HOMES FOR POOR PEOPLE

The very poor lived in overcrowded, badly-built slums, which had little ventilation, no proper drainage, and were often filthy. Many people died young in these unhealthy conditions.

Slum dwellings

Most poor families had to share one or two rooms in cramped, often damp and draughty houses. Some even lived in dark cellars.

The workhouse

The poorest families, who could not afford rent, went to the workhouse. Workhouses gave people food, work and a place to sleep, but families were separated and kept apart.

Some families slept, ate and worked in the same room.

Better housing

After 1875, many slums were pulled down. In big cities, new blocks of flats were built, often paid for by wealthy businessmen. These were rented out cheaply to tailors, porters, police constables, needlewomen, printers and other skilled workers.

An extract about Peabody Buildings from *The Life of George Peabody*

There were neatly tiled floors and whitewashed walls. The rooms were small, but planned economically... I noticed, especially, that each room was well lighted and ventilated. Some families had three rooms... Each floor is divided into lettered sections with spacious corridors. There are iron traps in the halls in each storey into which dirt and rubbish from each tenement [flat] is swept.

What does the writer like about Peabody Buildings?

Wealthy people and companies built almshouses – homes for poor, old people.

SUBURBS

City centres were noisy, smelly and dirty. The air was thick with smoke from factories and coal fires and there was little or no clean water. Those who could afford it moved out to suburbs on the edge of cities.

Victorian suburban railway station

Train services

Railway companies ran cheap, early morning trains for workers. Suburban stations were built for people to travel to work into city centres. Builders put up streets of cheap homes nearby for workers to live in.

Terraced homes

Workers' houses were built in long terraces. Each one had a parlour at the front, used only on Sundays and for guests. At the back were a kitchen, a scullery and a privy.

Upstairs were two or three bedrooms, but no bathroom. The houses all had back yards and some had tiny front gardens, as well.

Most Victorian terraced houses were built of brick. They were cheap to build because their side walls were shared.

Wealthier people lived in big detached houses, called villas, with large rooms, gardens and privacy from the street.

Look out for these common features of many Victorian houses.

Pillared doorways

Plaques showing the name of a house or the date it was built

Decorated wooden bargeboards with a finial on the top

Bay windows to let more light into a house

Lots of chimney pots

Iron railings outside the front garden

Boot scraper for wiping off mud from the streets

Coal hole covers on the pavement for houses with coal cellars

Sash windows that go up and down. They usually have only two or four glass panes.

COMFORTABLE HOMES

Victorian villas and town houses of the wealthy usually had three floors. Often there were attic rooms and a basement, as well. Families filled their rooms with dark furniture and lots of ornaments, and lined the walls with pictures.

Downstairs

The kitchen was tucked away in the basement or at the back of the house. On the ground floor were the parlour, the dining room and a study or library.

Upstairs

On the first floor were the main bedrooms and a drawing room where guests were entertained. On the top floor were the servants' bedrooms and a nursery for the children.

Houses were cold and draughty compared with modern ones. Rooms had thick, heavy curtains and open fireplaces.

Maids worked long hours. They got up before the family and often worked until 10pm.

Servants

Big homes like these employed servants. Some families had one maid of all work. Wealthy families had all sorts of servants – a housekeeper, a cook, kitchenmaids, housemaids and laundry maids.

A hard day's work

Maids had to keep a house spotless. They dusted and swept every room each morning. They filled jugs with hot water for washing. They cleaned and lit the kitchen range, polished boots, scrubbed the doorsteps, washed the windows, made the beds and laid and cleared the dining table. There were no vacuum cleaners, washing machines, fridges or electric kitchen gadgets, so everything in a house was done by hand.

Feather duster

Sacking duster

Boot brushes

Bar of soap

Cinder sifter for ashes

Bath brick for polishing the range

HEAT AND LIGHT

All homes, both rich and poor, were warmed with open fires. There were fireplaces in every room, which is why Victorian houses have so many chimneys.

Lumps of coal

Kitchen range

An extract from *Mrs Beeton's Book of Household Management*

She *[the cook]* should first clean out of the fireplace the remains of the fire of the night before, then thoroughly brush the range. For lighting the fire she will require some paper, firewood, a few lumps of round coal, some cinders and a few matches.

The fire being lighted, the cook should clear away all the ashes and cinders, rub up with a leather the brighter parts of the range and wash the hearth; when washed quite clean, but while it is still wet, she should rub it with a piece of hearthstone to whiten it, and place the kettle on the fire to boil.

How many tasks did a cook have to do before she could boil a kettle?

The kitchen range

A large, iron, coal-fired range in the kitchen heated an oven and hobs for cooking. Water was heated in a big kettle for tea, baths and washing up. People heated heavy flat irons on the range for ironing. Coal was added all day long to keep the fire burning.

Flat iron

Iron kettle

Lighting

For most of Queen Victoria's reign, houses were lit by oil lamps and, later, by gas light. Oil lamps gave out a very dim glow. Gas light was much brighter. Electric light bulbs were invented in 1879, but only the very rich had electricity in their homes by the end of the 19th century.

Bedtime

People lit their bedrooms with candles. In cold weather, they put a stone hot water bottle into their bed to warm up the sheets.

Oil lamp

The deep rim of the candlesticks caught any dripping wax.

Stone hot water bottle

This room in a late Victorian home is lit by gas light. Notice the extra oil lamp at the back.

WASHING AND BATHS

Early Victorian houses had no bathrooms, hot running water or inside loos. By the end of the century, families who could afford it put in bathrooms, but the poorest never took a bath at all.

Jug

Washing and bathing

In well-off houses, every bedroom had a washstand with a washbowl and jug. A servant brought up hot water in a can from the kitchen, and later carried the dirty water downstairs.

Washbowl

Chamber pots

Both adults and children kept chamber pots under their bed, in case these were needed at night. A servant emptied them every morning.

Metal hot water can

People took hip baths in front of a fire, surrounded by screens to keep out draughts. The water came up only to a bather's hips.

Washing for the poor

In poorer homes, people bathed once a week in a tin bath. Keeping clean was a struggle in the slums, because more than a dozen families might share a cold tap and a privy. Families rarely had a private place where they could wash and they often all used the same bath water.

Tin bath

Baths and wash-houses

After 1846, some big towns built public baths and wash-houses. Here, people could have hot or cold baths in private, with clean towels and soap. There were also laundry rooms for washing clothes and linen.

Baths and wash-houses had separate baths for men and women, and a plunge (swimming) pool, used mainly by men and boys.

FAMILIES

Victorian families were much larger than today's. Queen Victoria had four sons and five daughters and the average Victorian family had six children. By the end of the century, families became much smaller.

Fathers and mothers

In well-off families, the father was the head of the family and expected his wife and children to obey him. Fathers went out to work and spent little time with their children. Mothers did not need to work. They stayed in the house, organising servants, planning meals and creating a comfortable home.

Photographs often emphasise family roles. Here, the father and eldest son stand over the rest of the family. The eldest daughter sits next to her mother.

Everyone in this poor family is helping to make matchboxes.

Working families

In poorer homes, men were paid too little to support their family, so wives and children also had to work hard. Some families worked together at home, making boxes, brushes and other small things.

Children at work

Many children worked long hours in factories, mills or in the street, until laws were passed to prevent this. Even after schooling became compulsory, many children still worked, as well.

Extract from an interview with a headmaster in *Living London*

'He [the boy] was up at five o'clock this morning, and out with the milkman on his round. This evening he will be selling papers. You know, these poor children are not put to bed as early as yours are. They don't get a fair average of sleep for growing children, and when they have to work before and after school, to add a little to the family earnings, you can't expect them to have very much energy left for their work when they come to school. It is pitiful.'

Why does the headmaster feel sorry for poor children?

BABIES

Many mothers had a new baby year after year. They usually had their babies at home. There was little medical care. Many mothers died in childbirth and their babies often died, too.

Little mothers

In poor families, the older girls helped look after the babies and younger children. Many girls were kept back from school to help at home – especially on washday or when their mother went out to work.

These girls are helping their mother dress their younger sisters for going out.

An extract from
The Mother's Thorough Resource Book

The dress of an infant should be light, loose, easy, and warm. A belly-band of flannel should be worn for the first three or four months. It is a great preservative against colds. A petticoat is next required, which should be wide enough to wrap around the feet. An outer garment and a pair of knitted socks and cotton shirts complete the indoor wardrobe. For outdoor wear, a hood, robe, cape, veil and gloves will be added.

How does this baby clothing compare with that of today?

Nursemaids often started work as young as 14 years old.

Well-off families employed a live-in nanny who took total charge of the babies and young children. Some had a nursemaid as well. Nannies bathed, dressed, fed and looked after the children in the nursery. In big houses, there were two nurseries – one for daytime play and meals and one for bathing and sleeping at night.

Perambulators

Victorians thought that fresh air was healthy for babies. Nannies took them for daily rides in a perambulator.

HEALTH AND ILLNESS

In overcrowded towns, which had open drains and dirty water supplies, deadly diseases spread rapidly. For much of Queen Victoria's reign, frequent epidemics of cholera and typhoid killed thousands of people.

Dirty water

A report in 1842 revealed that more than half the towns in Britain had dirty water. In 1853, John Snow, a doctor, proved that cholera was spread by dirty water. Gradually, people recognised that clean water was essential for people's health. After 1875, pipes were laid to bring clean water straight into homes and sewers carried away waste. Rubbish collections also began, so streets became much cleaner.

The doctor's visit

Advertisement for a ready-made cure

Medical treatment

Doctors charged fees, so only the wealthy could afford a doctor's visit. Most people treated illnesses with home-made remedies or medicines from a chemist. Some of the ready-made cures were useless and advertisements for them made all sorts of untrue claims.

Free gift from the makers of Mrs Winslow's cough mixture

Children's health

Children, both rich and poor, often caught dangerous diseases, such as diphtheria, measles, smallpox, scarlet fever and whooping cough.

Early feeding bottles had long tubes, which were hard to clean. Germs collected in the tubes and made babies ill.

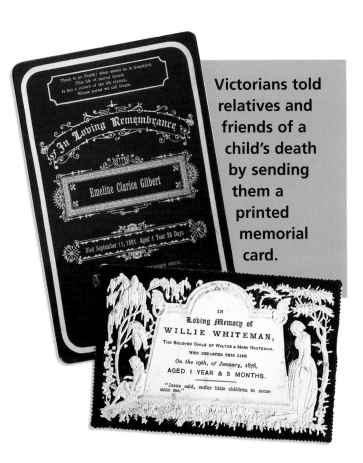

Victorians told relatives and friends of a child's death by sending them a printed memorial card.

Baby deaths

More than a quarter of all babies died before their first birthday. Many died from diarrhoea, caused by dirty milk or water. Some were accidentally poisoned by a drug given to keep them quiet. Many young children also died, especially those who were weak or underfed.

Extract from
The Book of the Home

BABY AILMENTS

Bronchitis When young babies get bronchitis it is owing to carelessness in keeping them out late at night, or exposing them to fog, east wind, or draughts while washing. The complaint is extremely dangerous. If all children from birth wore woollen underclothing with high necks, long sleeves and long stockings and had double-breasted flannel nightgowns or sleeping suits, the present very high death-rate among children from chest complaints would be reduced considerably.

What does this writer consider to be the causes of bronchitis and what cure is suggested?

CLOTHES

Rich and poor children wore very different clothes. Poor children had to wear ragged cast-offs. Wealthy children had new clothes especially made for them, copying adult fashions of the time.

Clothes for the very young

Babies and small children were often dressed in white. Little boys wore dresses until the age of five or six, when they were breeched (allowed to wear trousers). Girls grew their hair long and wore it loose or tied back with a ribbon.

The young children on the left are both boys. Sometimes, mothers let their boys' hair grow long, like the girls'.

Boys' fashion in the 1880s

Girls' and boys' clothes

Well-off girls wore shorter versions of their mothers' clothes. When they were about 16, they started wearing long skirts and put up their hair. Boys wore short trousers called breeches and white shirts with detachable collars, which could be removed for washing.

Girls' fashion in the 1870s

Detachable collar

Children wearing tartan   Boy in a sailor suit

Followers of fashion

The Royal family influenced children's fashion. In 1844, Queen Victoria and Prince Albert bought Balmoral Castle in Scotland and spent holidays there. The royal family often dressed in tartan and this encouraged other families to follow suit. Sailor suits became popular for boys after the Prince of Wales was painted in one.

When *Little Lord Fauntleroy* was published in 1886, it started a fashion for boys to wear velvet suits with white, lacy collars, like the character in the book.

Clothes washing

Clothes were washed by hand. This took several days. White clothes were boiled in a copper boiler over a coal fire. Other clothes were washed in a tub and scrubbed on a washboard. Wet clothes were wound through a mangle. This pressed out some of the water before the clothes were pegged out to dry.

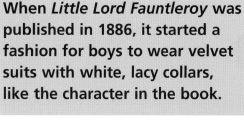
Copper boiler in a scullery

Flat iron

Ironing

Clothes were ironed with a flat iron. People used two irons – heating one up on the kitchen range, while they ironed with the other one.

Mangles were made of iron with heavy wooden rollers.

KEEPING IN TOUCH

At the start of Victoria's reign, the only way for people to keep in touch was by letter. The person who received a letter paid for the postage, which was costly and depended on how far a letter had travelled.

The Penny Post

In 1840, Rowland Hill invented the idea of postage stamps. The cost of sending a letter anywhere in the country was one penny. The first stamp was known as a 'Penny Black'. Post boxes were put on the streets and letter-carriers collected, sorted and delivered letters, just as postmen do today.

The Post Office persuaded people to fit letter boxes in their doors so letters could be delivered.

Postal districts

Streets were given name plates and houses numbers, so postmen knew where to deliver letters. To make sorting easier, big cities were gradually divided into postal districts.

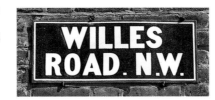

The first post boxes were green. In 1874, they were painted bright red. Notice the initials VR on the front. These stand for Victoria Regina ('regina' means queen in Latin).

Letters and greetings cards

With cheaper postage, many more people started sending letters. They also sent birthday, Christmas and fancy Valentine cards.

Postcards

In 1870, the Post Office introduced an official postcard with a stamp already printed on it. Postcards cost half the price of sending letters, so they soon became very popular. At first, postcards were plain, with room for the address on one side and a message on the back. Later, they were printed with pictures.

The first Christmas card was sent in 1843. Sending Christmas cards soon became a popular custom.

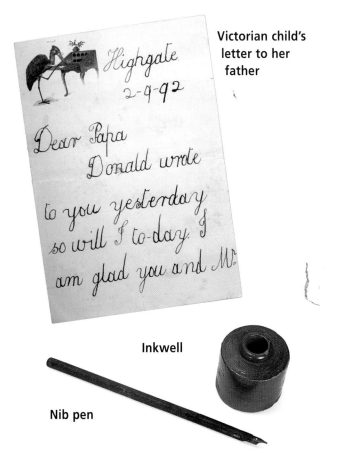

Victorian child's letter to her father

Inkwell

Nib pen

Writing

People wrote with pen and ink. Children learned to write in a style known as copperplate. Typewriters were invented in 1874. They were mainly used by businesses for bills, orders and letters.

Telegraph and telephone

In 1844, Samuel Morse invented a way of sending messages in a code of dots and dashes over electric telegraph wires. Operators translated the code into written messages known as telegrams. Telephones were invented in 1876, but they were not common in Victorian homes.

27

THE NURSERY

Children from well-off families lived in large houses with several rooms. The children spent most of their time in the nursery. This was both their schoolroom and their playroom. It was full of toys, games and books.

A room full of toys

Some of the toys Victorian children played with were the same as children's toys today. Look for the dolls, toy highchairs, model animals and the dolls' house. Most Victorian toys were made of wood or metal.

This is the reconstructed Victorian nursery in a grand house, called Lanhydrock, in Cornwall.

Toys for all tastes

Boys and girls were given different toys. Girls played with dolls, dolls' houses and miniature household equipment. Boys played with toy soldiers, trains or did science experiments.

Toy soldiers

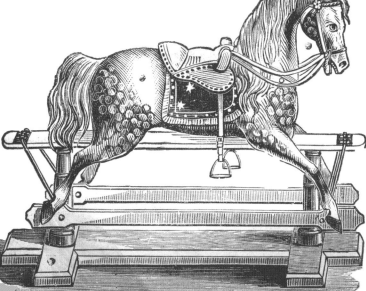

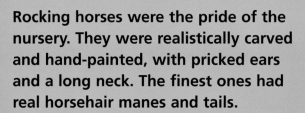

Rocking horses were the pride of the nursery. They were realistically carved and hand-painted, with pricked ears and a long neck. The finest ones had real horsehair manes and tails.

Books of all kinds

Until the middle of Queen Victoria's reign, most children's books were educational or told stern moral tales, such as *Struwwelpeter*. By the end of the 19th century, many more books were being written purely for children's amusement, such as *Treasure Island*, *The Jungle Book* and *Alice in Wonderland*. There were also illustrated nursery rhyme and picture books for younger children.

Books and magazines of the late 1800s

INDOOR PLAY

Well-off Victorian children amused themselves with board games, dressing up and performing plays, playing word games and learning tricks.

Table games

Children played traditional games, such as draughts, dominoes and solitaire, as well as new ones. The game of halma was invented in 1888. Players had to cross their playing pieces from one side of a board to the other. Tiddlywinks was another newly invented game. Players had to flip pieces from a table into a cup.

Father and son playing halma

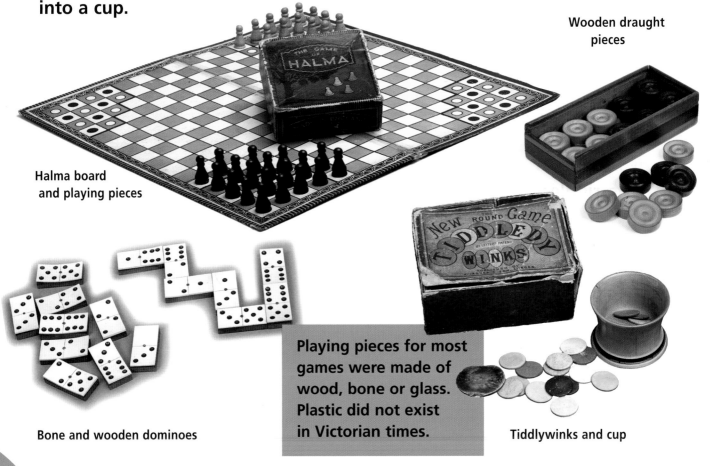

Wooden draught pieces

Halma board and playing pieces

Playing pieces for most games were made of wood, bone or glass. Plastic did not exist in Victorian times.

Bone and wooden dominoes

Tiddlywinks and cup

Book of games

Party games

At parties, children played games that are still played today, such as musical chairs, blind man's buff and Simon says. Charades was a very popular game, where people acted out words for other players to guess.

Tricks and puzzles

Many children were very keen on magic and scientific tricks, number puzzles, and word games such as guessing riddles, anagrams and proverbs. Children's magazines often included puzzle competitions.

Putting on plays

Some children and their friends enjoyed learning plays and performing them in front of their families. They dressed up and made their own props.

A puzzle from *A Book of Games*

SIX AND FIVE MAKE NINE
This is a simple little puzzle. Take eleven strips of cardboard, lay six of them at exactly equal distances on the table.

| | | | | |

Ask one of the company to add five other strips and yet only make nine. It is done by placing them as in the dotted lines, thus:

Script of a children's play

PASTIMES

Well-off families also entertained themselves at home with music, hobbies or shows.

Magic lanterns

Victorians invented all sorts of amusements. Magic lantern shows were popular at children's parties and at Christmas. Hand-painted glass slides were moved in front of the light of a lantern and projected on to a screen.

The beam of light in a magic lantern came from a gas or oil lamp.

People marvelled at being able to hear music on a machine.

Sounds and pictures

The gramophone was the first machine to play recordings on flat disks called records. The zoetrope was a toy which seemed to make pictures move. A strip of sequenced pictures was put into a drum with slits. When viewers looked through the slits as the drum was spinning, they saw only one 'moving' image.

Replica zoetrope and pictures

Making music

Wealthy and middle-class girls spent most of their day at home. Most households owned a piano and piano playing was considered an important accomplishment for girls. They played to entertain their family and guests.

Piano practice

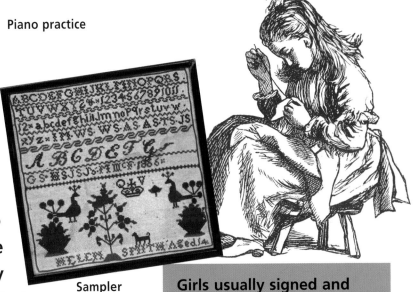

Needlework

Sewing was another skill that all girls were expected to learn. They spent a lot of time practising different stitches by making samplers, which included both letters and pictures.

Sampler

Girls usually signed and dated their sampler and included their age, as well.

Collections

Many children enjoyed cutting, arranging and pasting coloured scraps into a scrapbook. They bought the scraps in sheets, which had pictures joined by tabs. Others liked making collections of coins, stamps, postmarks, flowers or shells.

Victorian scrapbook and scraps

SUNDAYS

Sundays were seen by respectable Victorians as days of rest and prayer. Children were not allowed to play with their usual toys and games.

Quiet play

After going to church and Sunday School, children were expected to find quiet ways to amuse themselves during the long afternoon.

Children dressed in their best clothes on Sundays – girls often wore white dresses with frills and boys wore suits.

A Sunday toy

A Noah's ark was one of the only toys children were allowed to play with on Sundays, because it depicted a Bible story. Children could re-enact the story, lining up animals in pairs to go into the ark, to escape the coming flood. Often, however, children made up their own stories about the animals.

This ark and animals have been hand-carved from wood and painted in realistic, bright colours.

Sunday books

Some children's books and magazines were especially written to be read on Sundays. Many stories were religious; others were adventure or school tales with a moral. There were also poems to learn, competitions to enter and pages to colour. These books were often given to children as Sunday School prizes.

The cover of this Sunday book reminded children to give to others less fortunate than themselves.

Religious colouring picture

Bible reading

At the end of Sunday, families often gathered in the front room and the father read aloud from the Bible.

An extract from *The Children's Treasury of Pictures and Stories*, 1899

A little girl asked her mother, "Which is worse – to tell a lie or to steal?"

The mother, taken by surprise replied that both were so bad she couldn't tell which was worse.

"Well," said the little girl, "I've been thinking that it is worse to lie than to steal. If you steal a thing, you can take it back or pay for it, but a lie is for ever!"

OUTDOOR FUN

Country children spent much of their time outside. Wealthier city children had gardens to play in, but those from poor families had little fresh air or exercise.

City spaces

Drinking fountain

Industrial cities had become overcrowded and polluted, as more and more people came to them to work. People realised that these filthy surroundings were spreading disease, so they started widening streets and building public parks. The spacious parks meant that people could stroll in the fresh air. Many parks had drinking fountains, bandstands for musicians, a boating lake, benches and shelters.

Children play in a sandpit at this city park. Notice that all the boys are wearing caps and all the girls are wearing hats.

Country children

Most country children had to help with chores and farmwork and had little time for play. In their free time, they played with hoops, tops and marbles or roamed the fields, watching birds and wildlife.

Natural pleasures

Boys climbed trees in search of birds' nests, went fishing, followed animal tracks and made whistles and pop-guns from twigs. Girls collected flowers or played skipping and rhyming games.

The autumn was a time for picking nuts and blackberries, and for gathering mushrooms.

Cycling around

After bicycles were invented in the 1880s, cycling quickly became a popular sport. Roads, especially those in the country, were very safe and quiet for cyclists, because there were no cars.

Cycling map

Older boys joined cycling clubs that organised rides into the country.

SPORTS

Team sports, such as football, rugby and cricket, were played in boys' public schools, such as Eton, Harrow and Rugby. These schools were the first to organise these games and lay down a set of rules.

Footballers wore long-sleeved shirts with collars, long shorts and leather ankle boots.

Football

Children played football in the street or in fields, using a blown-up pig's bladder as a ball. The game was rough and rules varied. In 1863, some men got together and formed the Football Association. They agreed on definite rules. Some footballers became professionals – paid to play for a club. By the end of the century, watching football matches had become a popular activity.

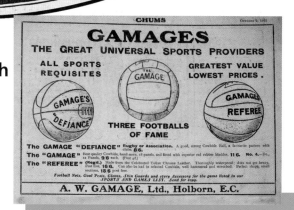

From the 1870s onwards, factories made leather footballs of a standard size and weight.

A game of cricket

Cricket

In early Victorian times, cricket was part of country life. It was played on village greens with a curved bat. The ball was bowled underarm and there were no real rules until 1835. Cricket became very popular among well-to-do boys at public schools, who continued playing once they grew up and formed cricket clubs.

Badminton

The modern sport of badminton started in 1893, when an association agreed a set of rules. It grew out of a popular children's game, called battledore and shuttlecock. Two players hit a shuttlecock (a small, feathered cork) to and fro with bats called battledores. They tried to keep the shuttlecock in the air for as many hits as possible.

Unlike badminton, battledore and shuttlecock did not need a net or a court. It was played in the street.

39

STREET GAMES

Children from poor families had very few toys and lived in small, overcrowded homes with no space to play indoors. Instead, they played games in the street.

Hopscotch

Skipping

A skipping rhyme
All in. A bottle of gin.
All out. A bottle of stout.
All in together.
Frosty weather.

Fun for free

Children used what they could find for their games. They skipped with a length of old rope. They scratched a hopscotch court in the ground. They hung a rope around a lamp-post as a swing. They played a game called five-stones, where they threw five pebbles into the air and tried to catch as many as possible on the back of one hand. They also played tag and leap-frog.

Leap-frog

Marbles

Boys liked playing with marbles. The cheapest ones were made from clay; others were made from stone or coloured glass. Lemonade bottles had clear glass marbles as stoppers. Children broke the bottles to get the marbles out.

Lemonade bottle

Boys dug a hole in the ground and tried to throw a handful of ten marbles into the hole at once.

Clay marbles

Whipping tops

A wooden whipping top was a cheap, popular toy to buy. A leather or string whip was wound around the cone-shaped top. Children put their top on the ground and quickly pulled away the whip. The child whose top kept spinning for the longest was the winner.

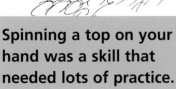

Spinning a top on your hand was a skill that needed lots of practice.

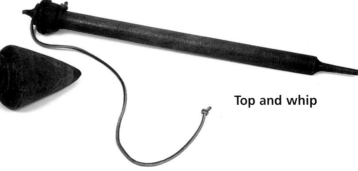

Top and whip

ENTERTAINMENT

All sorts of entertainers performed in the streets. There were musicians and shows, and, occasionally, a bear, which stood on its hind legs to dance.

Seasonal shows

Children only went to the theatre at Christmas, to see a pantomime with their family as a special treat. Sometimes they went to the circus. There was great excitement when, once a year, a travelling fair came to town with its steam-driven rides.

Punch and Judy shows took place on street corners. A drummer banged loudly to attract an audience.

Men wandered through busy streets, wearing boards like these, to advertise a pantomime.

Circus show

Poor children enjoyed dancing in the street for free, to the music of a barrel organ.

Street music

In large towns and cities, musicians filled the streets and markets with their tunes, hoping people would give them a penny or two. There were Scottish bagpipe players, Italian violinists and harpists, and barrel organ grinders, who often trained a tame monkey to collect money.

Military brass bands played free concerts at bandstands in parks and at the seaside.

OUTINGS

Children from well-off families sometimes went to places of interest as a special treat.

Picnics

In the summer, families went on picnics. Mrs Beeton, in her *Book of Household Management*, suggested a picnic menu for children of ham and beef sandwiches, cold meat rolls, fruit and jam puffs, cakes, fresh fruit, home-made lemonade, lime-juice cordials and water.

Family picnic

Educational visits

The Victorians were the first to build free public libraries, museums and zoos (known then as zoological gardens). Zoos gave children the chance to see live wild animals, such as bears, tigers, lions, monkeys and exotic birds. Natural history museums displayed stuffed animals, fossils, skeletons and rocks.

An elephant ride was the exciting highlight of a visit to the zoo.

Sunday School outings

The only treat that the poorest children ever had was a yearly Ragged School or Sunday School outing to the nearest patch of countryside or a day trip to the sea.

These pictures were on the front page of a newspaper, illustrating an article about a country outing for Ragged School children.

Children waiting for a tram-car

Long swing for the girls

Game of cricket for the boys

Extract from The *Daily Graphic*, August 28, 1891

Three or four mornings in every week, a little crowd of more or less ragged children may be seen on the pathway in Mile End Road waiting for the special tram-cars that will take them to the borders at Epping Forest.

MARCHING INTO THE FOREST
Arrived at Walthamstow, the crowd of fully a hundred children is formed into a procession and they march onwards to the 'retreat'. Here in a canvas-roofed shed, decorated with illuminated texts, the long wooden tables are spread with cups and plates for breakfast. But before they begin, the director has a few words about the love of God, the evils of drink and of kindness to one another.

ROMPING ON THE GREEN
After breakfast there are two roundabouts and two long swings – one for boys and one for girls; cricket balls and stumps, hoops and toys of all sorts are distributed and play begins in earnest. They are a troublesome little crowd. "They won't let me play with them." "This boy hit me." "He's took my hoop."

Why do you think this outing was reported in a newspaper?
- What games were provided for the children?
- What else were they given?
- What did the director talk about to them? Why did he do this?

HOLIDAYS

The main holidays that people celebrated were Easter, May Day, Whitsun and Christmas.

May Day

On May Day (1st May), children in villages chose a girl to be the May Queen. They made a large garland of flowers and paraded with it, dressed in their best clothes. They stopped at houses to sing a song and ended the day with a huge tea. Another May Day custom was to dance around a maypole, holding brightly coloured ribbons.

Dancing around a maypole on May Day happened even in some city schools.

Children from each Sunday School marched behind their own banner.

Whitsun

Whitsun was a religious holiday, but it also marked the beginning of summer. Children were bought new clothes – girls got a straw hat with ribbons and boys got a new jersey or pair of trousers. Many children wore their new clothes to go on a Whitsun Walk with their Sunday School. All the Sunday Schools in a town joined together in a procession, with their embroidered banners flying.

Christmas time

Many Christmas traditions, such as sending cards, decorating the house and putting up a fir tree, carol singing, pulling crackers, eating turkey and Father Christmas, started in Victorian times.

Boxing Day

Boxing Day (26th December) got its name because this was the day when wealthy people gave boxes of gifts to their servants, and small sums of money to tradesmen who regularly called at their house.

Victorian
Christmas cards

What toys is Father Christmas carrying?
- Which of these toys might children receive now?
- How does the image of Father Christmas differ today?

THE SEASIDE

Only the well-off went to the seaside in early Victorian times. Poor families were not paid for time off work, so they could not afford holidays. After Bank Holidays began in 1871, workers took day trips to the seaside.

Weston-super-Mare

Resorts with railway lines grew rapidly as workers started to come by train on day trips.

On the beach

Holidaymakers sat on the beach and paddled in the sea, just as people do today. Everyone kept their clothes on and wore a hat. Women changed for swimming inside a hut on wheels called a bathing machine, which was pushed into the sea. There were entertainments and shellfish, lemonade and ice cream stalls.

How do these seaside activities from 1890 differ from those today?

Sitting on deck chairs

Drying clothes

Bathing machine

Punch and Judy show

Paddling

Barrel organ and monkey

Donkey rides

Picture postcards started in 1894. They showed seaside scenes with a pier and promenade – the pride of every big resort.

Seaside attractions

Every resort had a seafront promenade, where people could stroll and show off their best clothes. Some also had a Winter Garden, a building with a glass roof, where people could eat and dance in bad weather. Other attractions were aquariums, gardens with bandstands, boating lakes and souvenir shops.

People could watch a show and have a meal in the pavilion at the end of the pier.

The pier

Big resorts had a long, cast-iron pier. People paid a few pence to enjoy a breezy walk over the sea and watch entertainers.

49

CHILD WORKERS

Large numbers of Victorian children had to work to help their families with everyday costs, such as food and rent.

What differences do you notice between these rich children and the poor ones below?

Rich children

Children born into rich families did not work and lived in comfortable homes. They were warm, well-dressed and had enough to eat. Boys went to school and girls were taught at home, and they all had time for play.

Poor children

Poor children were not so lucky. Their parents sent them out to work as young as six, so that the family earned enough money for food. Children worked long hours, often in terrible conditions, in textile mills, down mines, in brickyards, on farms or selling things in the street.

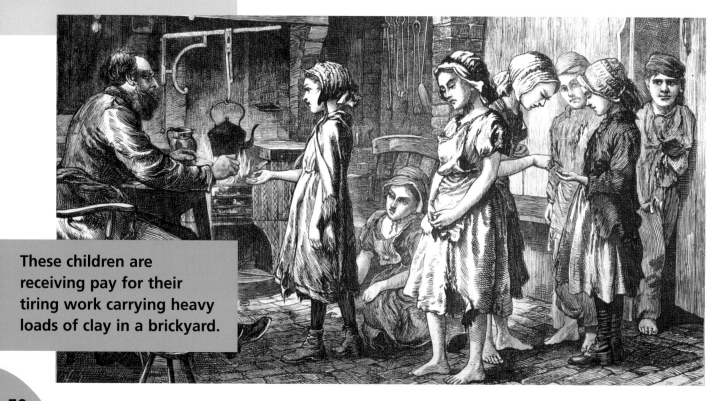

These children are receiving pay for their tiring work carrying heavy loads of clay in a brickyard.

Cotton mills

Cotton mill owners mainly employed women and children, because they did not have to pay them as much as men. Many of the children were orphans, who lived as well as worked at the mill. They worked for more than twelve hours a day, six days a week, every week of the year.

Full of danger

Cotton mills were unhealthy places to work. Windows were kept closed to prevent the thread from drying and snapping. Thick clouds of cotton dust made it hard to breathe. The machines had no guards, so children often had terrible accidents, getting limbs, hair or clothes caught in the whirling cogs and gears.

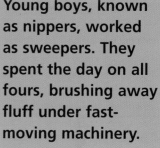

Young boys, known as nippers, worked as sweepers. They spent the day on all fours, brushing away fluff under fast-moving machinery.

Clogs worn by a child worker

NASTY JOBS

In the early Victorian period, it was accepted that poor children should work. There were few laws controlling working hours or conditions.

The Earl of Shaftesbury

Coal mines

Some of the worst places children worked were coal mines. The children developed twisted limbs from pushing the heavy coal wagons. They had breathing problems from the poisonous gases and dust they inhaled. Some died in explosions and accidents.

Studying children at work

Lord Ashley (who later became the Earl of Shaftesbury) persuaded Parliament to send commissioners to find out about children's work. They published reports which included interviews with children. The report on mines had drawings like this one below, which greatly shocked the public.

In mines, older children worked as 'putters'. They filled and pushed the coal wagons along rails to the mine shaft.

Younger children worked as 'trappers'. They sat for ten hours a day alone in dark, wet tunnels. They opened doors to let wagons through and to let fresh air into the mine.

Chimney brush and poles

Chimney sweeps sent small boys up twisting chimneys to sweep them. The boys got lung diseases and sometimes fell. A law banned children from chimney sweeping in 1875.

Ellison Jack, an eleven-year-old coal-carrier, interviewed for the Royal Commission of Children in Mines, 1842

I have been working below three years on my father's account. He takes me down to the mine at 2 *[o'clock]* in the morning and I come up at 1 or 2 the next afternoon. I go to bed at 6 at night to be ready next morning. I have to bear my burden *[load of coal]* up four traps or ladders, before I get to the main road that leads to the pit bottom. My task is four to five tubs; each tub holding four-and-quarter hundredweight *[equal to 50 kilos]*. I fill five tubs in 20 journeys. I have had the strap *[been beaten]* when I did not do my bidding. I am glad when my task is wrought *[finished]* as it sore fatigues me.

What was Ellison's job like?

- How many hours did she work a day?
- How heavy were her tubs of coal?
- What happened if she did not do enough work?

New laws

After these reports, the government passed a Mines Act in 1842, which banned all girls and boys under the age of ten from working in mines. Another act reduced children's working day in textile mills to ten hours. Inspectors visited mills to check the laws were obeyed.

ON THE FARM

Farmers struggled to make a living and needed children's earnings and help to support their families. Farm children always spent part of the year working, even when school became compulsory.

Seasonal work

Children went to school mainly in the autumn and winter when there was not much farm work to do. They stayed at home during hay making and harvest in the summer, when everyone lent a hand to get the crops in.

Harvest holidays

Schools tried to set summer holidays at harvest time. However, the harvest relied on the weather – if the harvest was late, children did not go to school until it was finished.

The men cut the hay with scythes. The women and older girls turned it with rakes to help it dry.

School log book entries

May 8
Poor attendance. Many children employed looking after cows and sheep.

June 3
Attendance scanty owing to children being wanted to assist with sheep shearing.

June 23
Many older children absent this week in consequence of hay making.

August 23
School breaks up today for the harvest holidays – for three weeks if harvest be over – otherwise for a month.

September 13
Attendance poor. It will not improve until the corn harvest is over.

November 7
Thin attendance, as so many children are potato digging.

Children's farm jobs throughout the year

Rattle used for bird scaring

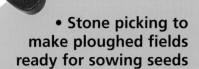

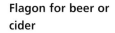
Flagon for beer or cider

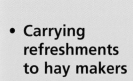

Sheaf

- Stone picking to make ploughed fields ready for sowing seeds

- Weeding fields by hand

- Bird scaring

- Planting potatoes

- Minding sheep and pigs

- Carrying refreshments to hay makers

- Vegetable and fruit picking

- Making bands for corn sheaves

- Gleaning (picking up leftover ears of wheat for using as animal feed or for grinding into flour for bread)

(March–May) **SPRING**

SUMMER (June–August)

(December–March) **WINTER**

AUTUMN (September–November)

- Collecting windblown branches and twigs as extra firewood

- Gathering carrots, turnips and potatoes

- Cleaning turnips for animal feed

- Feeding cows and pigs inside

- Collecting acorns as food for pigs

- Picking potatoes

- Minding pigs

- Bird scaring for autumn-sown crops

- Berry picking

Find out which of these farm jobs are still done today.

IN THE HOME

The most common job for girls, especially for those from the country, was as domestic (home) servants. The census of 1891 recorded 1.4 million female servants – more than 100,000 of them girls aged between ten and fourteen.

Servants' duties

Very rich households employed many servants, each with a specific job. Young girls started as scullerymaids, housemaids, nursemaids or laundry maids. They might progress to become cooks, housekeepers or nannies.

Scullerymaids cleaned everything in the kitchen and helped to prepare food.

Nursemaids helped to look after young children.

Housemaids dusted, swept, polished and scrubbed all the other rooms in the house.

Laundry maids washed and ironed clothes and bed linen.

Maids wore a uniform – a print dress for their morning work, and a black dress and a white apron and cap for greeting visitors in the afternoons.

HOUSEMAIDS BOX AND TRAY

An extract from *Mrs Beeton's Book of Household Management*, 1861

This is a list of what Mrs Beeton expected a maid to do before breakfast!
• Open the shutters and windows.
• Brush the range and light the fire.
• Clear away the ashes and clean the hearth.
• Polish the bright parts of the range.
• Put on the kettle.
• Sweep the dining room.
• Clean the grate and dust the furniture.
• Lay the table cloth for breakfast.
• Sweep the hall and shake the mats.
• Clean the doorstep.
• Polish the door knocker.
• Clean the boots.
• Bring the hot water urn into the dining room.
• Cook bacon, kidneys, fish, etc.

Maid of all work

Most girls had a hard, lonely life as a maid of all work – the only servant in a house. They got up at 6am and often worked until midnight. They were badly paid and had little time off, but they were usually well fed. All their work was done by hand, because there were no electric machines for cooking, cleaning or washing.

Which jobs still need doing in houses today?

Hot water and coal

Maids had a great deal of fetching and carrying to do. Hot water had to be heated on a coal-fired range and carried upstairs in cans for baths and washing. Coal had to be brought upstairs for the fires on every floor.

Hot water can   Coal hod

COTTAGE INDUSTRIES

Plaited straw hat

All over the country, young children worked in cottage industries, making things by hand.

Village handicrafts

In some villages, girls learned straw plaiting, or lace or glove making from the age of five or six. Either their mothers taught them or they went to classes, where teachers kept the children working hard, sometimes for ten hours a day.

Plaiting classes were held in local cottages. Sometimes as many as 30 children were crammed inside small rooms which had poor lighting, no heating and no fresh air.

Straw plaiting

At straw-plaiting schools, parents bought the children bundles of split straws. The children had to plait at least 20 metres of straw each day. The plaited straw was sold to hat makers for making into hats and bonnets.

Plaiting School

This girl is helping her mother, who is a box maker.

Homeworkers

In cities, many poor women took on work that could be done at home. They made paper bags, sweet wrappers, matchboxes, artificial flowers and Christmas crackers. Some wrapped up hairpins, sewed hooks and eyes onto display cards or hand-painted greetings cards.

Nimble fingers

The workers were paid by the number of things they made, not by their time, so their children all helped. As one mother said, 'Of course, it's hard on the little ones, but their fingers are so quick – they that has the most of 'em is the best off.'

Extract from
Recollections of a School Attendance Officer by John Reeves

They [working children] never played as children play, they never seemed to think as children. They were prematurely [too soon] old and the victims of awful cruelty.

SHOP BOYS

Milk measuring cups

Victorian shops were small and run by their owners. Bakers, grocers and butchers employed assistants and delivery boys to help them.

Delivery boys

There were no fridges in Victorian times, so people bought meat and groceries daily. Wealthy and middle-class people did not go shopping for food. Instead, delivery boys went to their houses collecting orders from the cook. Once the shopkeepers had made up the orders, the boys helped deliver the parcels to each house.

The butcher is giving his delivery boy orders for the day.

Milk delivery

By the middle of Victoria's reign, fresh milk was sent in churns from farms to towns by train. Boys helped delivery men take a churn on a cart around the streets. They measured out milk from metal cups into people's cans or jugs.

Milk delivery was done by horse cart like this, or by handcart, pulled by the delivery men.

Boys who worked in food shops wore long aprons over their clothes.

Shop life

Young boys were used as 'barkers'. They stood outside shops, shouting out prices and praising the goods on sale. The shop assistants lived above the shop and worked hard. Shops were open every weekday until 10pm and on Saturdays until midnight. The assistants were not allowed to sit down and always had to look clean and neat to give customers a good impression.

What qualities did shopkeepers look for in their assistants?

61

STREET SELLERS

Children from very poor families and homeless orphans often became street sellers. They mainly sold small, cheap, useful, everyday things.

Matchgirl

Tiring work

Children as young as six went out selling. They did not dare go home until they had earned enough money for the day. They worked long hours, often up to midnight, in all weathers, sometimes seven days a week.

An interview with a flower seller from Henry Mayhew's *London's Labour and the London Poor*

I have no relation in the world. I met a young woman in the street... who advised me to take up flower selling, as I could get nothing else to do. She showed me to market with her and showed me how to bargain with the salesman for flowers. At first when I went out to sell, I felt so ashamed I could not ask anyone else to buy of me.

- Why did this girl start selling flowers?
- Why might she have felt ashamed?

Girls sold bunches of flowers, watercress and lavender, or oranges.

Newsboys

Henry Mayhew, a journalist, discovered children selling things like these on the street.

Clothes pegs

Steel pen

Nutmeg grater

Newsboys

Boys sold newspapers on the street. At a time when there was no television or radio, newspapers were printed three times a day to give people the latest news. The bigger the story – such as a murder, a football match or a flood – the more newspapers the boys sold.

Costerboys

Costermongers, who sold fruit and vegetables from barrows, employed boys to shout out prices in their loud, shrill voices. The boys also helped to pull the barrows from street to street.

Costerboy

GUTTERSNIPES

In big towns, poor and homeless boys, known as guttersnipes or street urchins, did all sorts of odd jobs to scratch a living.

This cartoon shows how desperate boys fought to get a horse cab for a waiting gentleman.

Anything for a penny

Boys carried luggage to and from train stations, delivered parcels or ran messages. They held horses while their owners went into shops or visited houses. Some were link-boys, who lit the way with flaming torches for people out late at night.

Passers by gave small change to boys who performed acrobatics, played music or sang on street corners.

Link-boys led people through the dense fogs that often shrouded big cities.

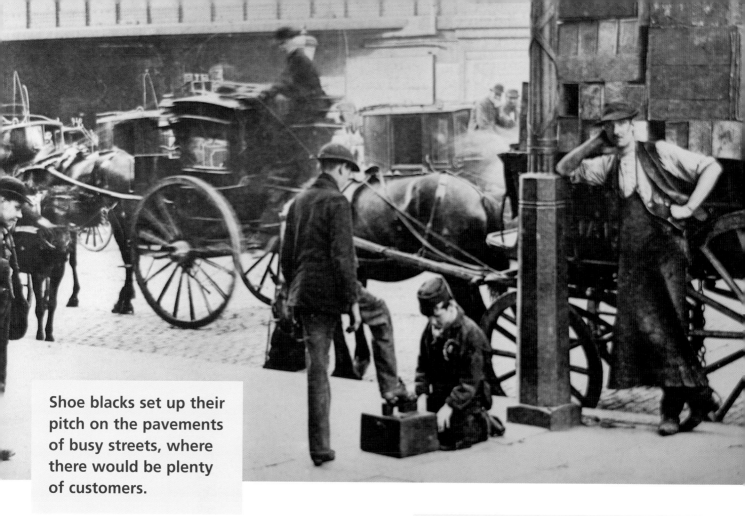

Shoe blacks set up their pitch on the pavements of busy streets, where there would be plenty of customers.

Shoe blacks

Some boys had more regular work. In 1851, the Earl of Shaftesbury set up the London Shoe Black Brigade to help children who shined shoes. The boys were given a uniform – a cap, an apron and a coloured jacket to show the area where they worked. In the evenings, they went to a Ragged School where they learned to read and write.

Crossing sweepers

Boys also worked at road junctions as crossing sweepers. Each one had a particular spot where he worked.

Rich people paid crossing sweepers to sweep away mud and horse dung, so that their polished shoes and long skirts would not get dirty.

SCAVENGERS

The poorest children of all scavenged for rubbish. They collected anything that could be resold and reused.

Rat poison bottle

Useful finds

Scavengers in the street were known as pickers-up. Their finds included bones, pieces of string, old iron, scraps of paper, broken crockery, empty tins, buttons, wire, pieces of wood, boot heels, medicine and other bottles, and damaged milk cans and saucepans.

Earnings

Many pickers-up were homeless. They spent the money they earned on a cheap lodging-house, bread and tea.

The children sorted their finds and sold them to specialist dealers or on a market stall.

Mudlarks

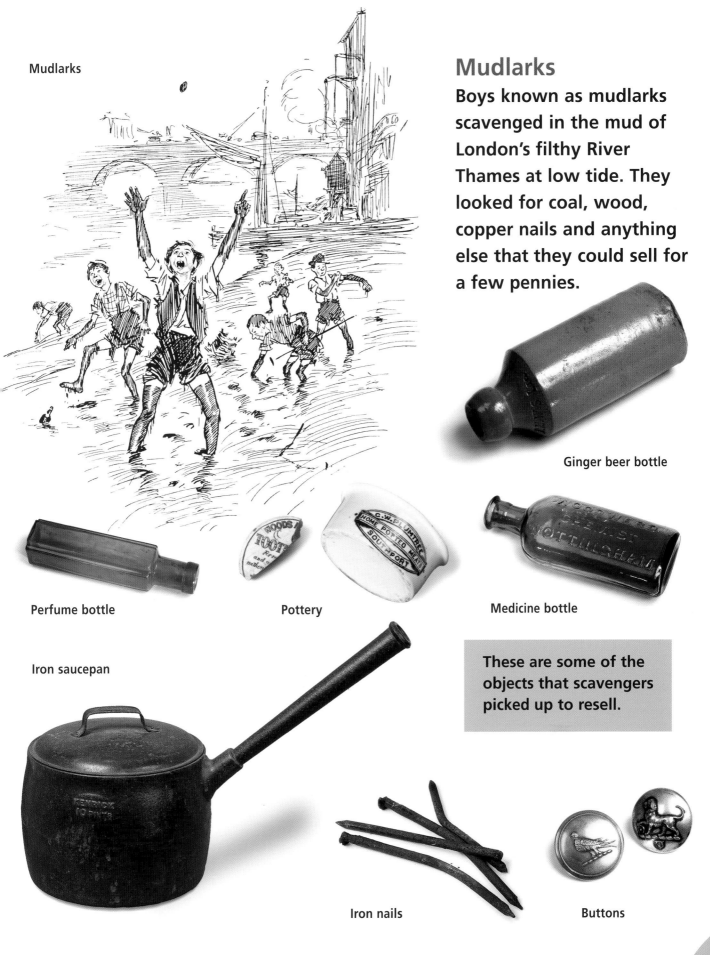

Mudlarks

Boys known as mudlarks scavenged in the mud of London's filthy River Thames at low tide. They looked for coal, wood, copper nails and anything else that they could sell for a few pennies.

Ginger beer bottle

Perfume bottle

Pottery

Medicine bottle

Iron saucepan

These are some of the objects that scavengers picked up to resell.

Iron nails

Buttons

HELPING CHILDREN

Many Victorians became very worried about children who had no families, homes or regular work, and who were often forced to beg or steal to survive.

Schools and refuges

In large towns, Ragged Schools were set up to teach poor children for free. These often provided meals and clothing as well as lessons. Wealthy people funded refuges where orphans could live and learn 'an honest trade'.

The boys at this school learned to sew, so they had a chance to become tailors when they grew up.

Girls of different ages lived together in the 50 cottages of the Village Home, looked after by a 'mother'.

Dr Barnado

Thomas Barnado was a doctor who lived and worked in the poor East End of London. He was horrified to discover homeless children sleeping on roofs, huddled against chimneys to keep warm.

A home for girls

Barnado opened homes for these children, including a Village Home for Girls. The girls were trained to be servants. On their 13th birthday, they left to work. The best pupils were given a maid's uniform to take with them.

EARLY SCHOOLS

When Queen Victoria came to the throne in 1837, there was no law that said children had to go to school.

Governess

Learning or work

Most rich and middle class boys went to private schools, which charged fees, but girls and young boys were generally taught at home by a governess. Many poor children did not go to school at all. They worked from an early age although some children learned to read and write at the factory where they worked.

Many churches and chapels had Sunday Schools which taught children to read so they could learn about the Bible. Some of them also ran classes during the week.

Even alphabet books were based on the Bible.

Schools for the poor

In villages, some young children went to a Dame school where an old woman – the 'dame' – taught them in her own home.

In poor areas of big cities, hundreds of Ragged Schools gave free schooling to very poor and often homeless children. The author Charles Dickens described these children as 'too ragged, wretched, filthy and forlorn' to enter any other place.

Children learned basic reading and writing at a Dame school. Parents paid a few pence each week.

The first Ragged Schools were set up in disused stables, lofts and railway arches. They often provided food and shelter as well as schooling.

Victorian pennies

FIELD LANE RAGGED SCHOOL.

SCHOOLS FOR ALL

In 1870, Parliament passed a law called the Education Act that said school places should be available for all children up to the age of ten.

Board schools

Groups of people were elected on to School Boards to set up new schools in their area. These were paid for by the rates (a local tax). Hundreds of new Board Schools were built, particularly in towns and cities. These huge, impressive buildings towered above the surrounding houses. Some had as many as 1,000 pupils. Parents had to pay a few pence a week for their children to attend until 1891, when schooling was made free.

Boys, girls and infants

Infants – aged 5 to 7 – were taught on the ground floor. After the age of 7, boys and girls were taught separately. Boys' classrooms were on the first floor and girls' classrooms were on the top floor. Boys and girls had separate playgrounds with a high wall between them. Some schools in built-up areas also had a playground on the roof.

Boys and girls had separate entrances, often marked in stone above the gate.

Look out for these features of Board Schools:

- two or more floors
- large, tall windows
- school board, school name and date plaques
- chimneys for the coal-fired stoves that heated classrooms on very cold days
- a high surrounding wall or railings
- separate entrances for boys, girls and infants
- playgrounds surrounded by high brick walls

Few people owned clocks or watches. A bell rang to tell children it was time for school to start.

THE CLASSROOM

Classrooms were crowded with up to 60 children. The huge windows let in as much light as possible, and gas lamps were lit on gloomy days. High ceilings helped to ventilate the room and let gas fumes escape.

How does your classroom compare with this one?

- How are the desks arranged?
- Where does your teacher sit?
- What equipment do you use?
- What is on the walls?
- What does the teacher write on?

The classroom layout

Children sat at desks, arranged in long rows, facing the teacher's desk at the front. The floor was stepped so that children in the back rows could see the blackboard and the teacher, and the teacher could keep an eye on the whole class at once.

Desks and benches

The wooden benches and desks were screwed to the floor. Hinged flaps on the desks could be raised for reading lessons and laid flat for writing on. Notice the slot for storing a slate, the inkwell, the shelf underneath for books and the sloping foot rest.

Slate

Inkwell

The pupils

Pupils had to sit still with straight backs, with their hands on their laps or behind their backs, if they were listening to the teacher. They were not allowed to talk unless a teacher asked them a question.

75

LEARNING TO WRITE

Sand tray

Pupils all learned the same thing at the same time. They copied down, word for word, what the teacher wrote on the blackboard or read out to them.

The children learned to write the alphabet one letter at a time.

Drawing in sand

Infants learned to write by drawing letters in a tray of sand. They drew in the sand with their fingers. The sand could be smoothed over and used again.

Slates

Once children knew their letters, they wrote on slates with a thin slate pencil. Paper was costly, but slates could be wiped clean and used again. Children were supposed to use a damp rag to clean their slate, but most used spit and their sleeve instead.

Slate and slate pencil

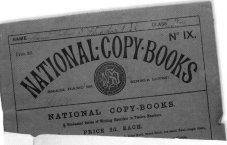

Copybook with proverbs

Copybooks

Older children used pen and ink. They copied sentences printed in a copybook word for word. Pupils all wrote exactly the same way, in a sloping style known as copperplate.

Teachers gave dictation. Children had to write down what the teacher read out, spelling tricky words correctly.

The split steel pen nibs often got crossed and dripped ink. Children were punished if they made ink blots in their copybooks.

Dictation exercise

I know no one who does not like **new** clothes.

He thought he **knew** more than any one else.

Then they **knew** it was of **no** use to **know** that.

Do you **know** now how I **knew** those were not **new**?

We **know no new** way to learn to read.

OTHER SUBJECTS

Once Board Schools were well established, more interesting lessons were introduced.

Blacksmith

Object lessons

Infant children had object lessons. The teacher held up an object or a picture and asked children questions about it. Some object lessons were about common things such as a bird's egg, a lead pencil, a candle or an apple. Others were about more unusual topics, such as horsehair, glue, whalebone, a railway carriage or a blacksmith's shop.

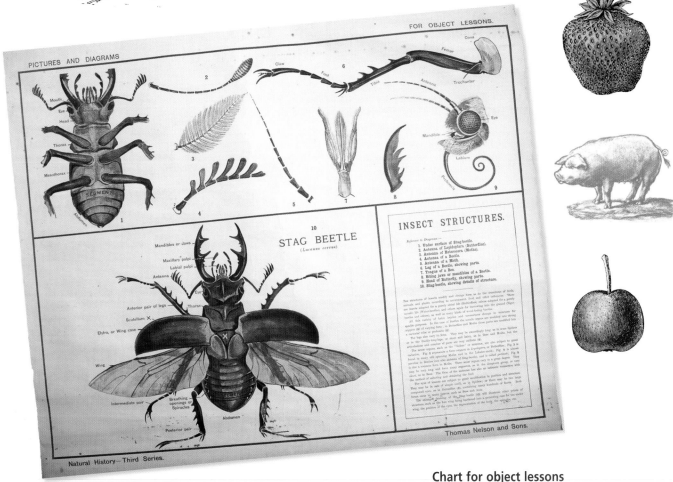

Chart for object lessons

Skills for jobs

Some older children went to schools where they learned useful skills. Boys learned printing, shoemaking and tailoring. Girls went to a house-wifery centre where they learned how to lay a fire, clean and polish a house, darn and patch clothes, to do the laundry and look after babies.

Special schools

By the end of Victoria's reign, children who were blind, deaf or disabled could go to special schools.

Boys learned how to make shoes and clothes by hand.

Blind boys learned useful skills for jobs, such as basket making, chair caning, mat making and sewing.

BOYS' LESSONS

The Victorians thought that boys should be taught useful skills for jobs they might have in the future. In the afternoons, the older boys at Board Schools had different lessons from girls.

Drawing class

Drawing copybook

Boys were taught to draw in a precise, technical way. They learned to draw by copying simple shapes, patterns and objects printed in a drawing copybook. Then they practised drawing objects, such as pyramids, cones, cubes and vases, arranged on a table in front of them. Everyone's drawings looked much the same.

Later, boys learned to make working drawings for their woodwork models.

Workshops were light, airy and well-equipped.

Workshops

From 1885, workshops known as Manual Training Centres were built in the playground of many Board Schools. Older boys learned to use woodwork tools, such as those shown on the right, to help them become skilled with their hands. Some boys also learned gardening.

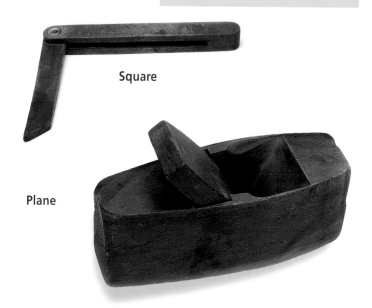

Square

Plane

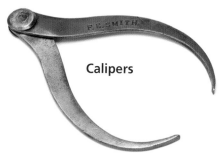

Calipers

This sign is over a doorway that led to a Manual Training Centre (M–T–C).

GIRLS' LESSONS

The Victorians thought girls should know how to be good housewives and mothers, so schools taught girls home-making skills.

By the time girls left school, they had learned to make petticoats, nightshirts, a girl's frock and a man's shirt.

Girls practised their stitching by making miniature clothes before they made real ones.

Sewing skills

It was thought to be essential to teach girls needlework, so they knew how to make and mend clothes. Girls spent four hours a week learning to stitch, hem, seam and make buttonholes. They had to sew with tiny, even stitches. Mistakes had to be unpicked and the sewing done again. Once a year, an examiner checked what the girls had made.

Cookery

Older girls learned cookery, and how to shop for food, at cookery centres built in the grounds of some schools.

Laundry work

There were no washing machines in Victorian times, so girls learned how to wash and starch clothes by hand. They also practised using different sorts of irons.

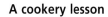
A cookery lesson

An extract from a textbook on laundry work

WASH DAY

Rise early! We can do more in one hour in the early morning than in two in the afternoon. The air is fresher and contains less smoke and dust and we are stronger. Light the boiler fire and a good supply of hot water.

1st Get out the dirt. Soak, wash, ie rub and rinse well.

2nd Keep everything a good colour. To keep the colour in white things, boil, blue and dry in the open air. To keep the colour in coloured things, wash and dry quickly.

Wash board for scrubbing clothes against

Soap

Flat irons

This is some of the equipment that girls learnt to use in laundry work.

Goffering tongs for shaping frills

Trivet for hot iron

Clothes pegs

EXERCISE AND HYGIENE

At fee-paying schools with large grounds, pupils played team sports, such as rugby, football and cricket. At Board Schools, which had small playgrounds, the only exercise children did was drill.

Dumb-bells

Drill

During drill, pupils lined up in rows in the playground and a teacher shouted commands. The children had to jump, bend or stretch in perfect time together. Sometimes, they lifted clubs or dumb-bells. Teachers thought that drill was a good way of teaching children how to obey orders, as well as giving them exercise.

Once a year, some schools performed a drill display at the Royal Albert Hall in London.

In cold weather, boys wore their jackets and caps for drill.

This teacher is checking children's scalps for ringworm. Children with dirty heads, sores, or rashes were sent home, so they did not infect the others.

Keeping clean

Poor pupils often came to school unwashed and in dirty clothes. The teachers' first job every day was to make sure children's hands and faces were clean and that they were not showing signs of illness.

Health and illness

Poor children often had sore eyes, matted hair and rotten teeth. They rarely owned hairbrushes or toothbrushes. Small, weak and underfed, these children easily caught diseases, such as smallpox, diphtheria, typhoid and scarlet fever, that are much rarer now. Some died. During an epidemic, a school was closed, sometimes for weeks. Headteachers kept a record of illnesses in a log book.

Log book entries

September 2
Several children absent through whooping cough in the house.
September 9
A great deal of sickness prevails, especially measles.
November 10
A few cases of scarlet fever.

Have you or any of your classmates had any of these illnesses?

ABSENCES

When Board Schools first started, it was hard to persuade poor parents to send their children to school. They needed children to work. Until schools became free, many families could not afford or refused to pay for schooling.

Mini-mothers
Girls often stayed at home on washday or to look after their brothers and sisters.

Reward card

Headteachers encouraged pupils to be punctual by giving reward cards to those who turned up on time all term.

Pupils who attended school regularly were rewarded with book prizes.

Attendances

School Boards paid a grant to schools for every day that a child attended. If attendance was low, schools received less money. Headteachers were keen to make sure children came to school regularly. They had to keep a record of weekly attendance in their log book, which was inspected once a year.

Attendance officers

School Boards hired attendance officers to track down children who should have been at school.

Pupils who never missed a single day at school for several years running were rewarded with Queen Victoria medals.

Which of these reasons for absence might still be accepted today?

Log book entries

January 13
Attendance affected by dense fog.

February 22-27
Attendance exceedingly low, affected by a severe snowstorm. Many of our children are ill booted, clothed and fed.

April 26-May 3
The fine weather of the past week seems to keep down attendance in the upper class.

May 9
Frequently the boys who play truant go into the park to pick up the ball for the gentlemen playing cricket. Others go about picking up iron to sell at the marine stores dealer.

June 28
Several were absent this week owing to haymaking having commenced.

July 5
Several Sunday School treats this week have interfered with the attendance of many children.

August 23
Several girls are still in the country and a few have gone hop picking.

PUNISHMENTS AND REWARDS

Teachers tried to make pupils work hard, behave well and arrive on time by being very strict. Pupils were usually very scared of their fierce teachers.

Cane

Being caned

Children who talked or laughed in class, made spelling mistakes, ink blots or disobeyed the teacher were beaten with a thin, bendy birch cane.

Punishment book

Headteachers kept a record of canings in a punishment book. Girls were caned only across the hand. Boys were often caned across their bottoms.

Boy wearing a dunce's cap a punishment for poor work

Punishment book entries

Name of child	Age	Offence	Punishment
Kathleen Scott	9	Disobedience	2 strokes
Elizabeth Kybert	9	Lying	4 strokes
Ada Horne	13	Impertinence	4 strokes
Rose Harwood	7	Laziness and temper	2 strokes
Beatrice Lewis	8	Continual lateness	2 strokes
Mabel Archer	10	Obstinacy	3 strokes
Edith Turner	9	Talking and playing	4 strokes
Florence Cook	8	Whistling in class	2 strokes
Florence Gray	8	Truanting	6 strokes
Kathleen Scott	9	Vulgarity	2 strokes
May Piggott	9	Scribbling in book	2 strokes
May Reed	8	Cheating	2 strokes
Louisa Jones	10	Playing with gas	4 strokes
Elsie Scott	13	Careless work	1 stroke
Bertha Gooby	8	Eating in school	2 strokes
Alice Staines	7	Playing with ink	1 stroke
Nelly Harwood	8	Very untidy work	1 stroke

Compare these entries in a punishment book.

- Were pupils punished more for bad behaviour or for poor work?
- What was considered the worst offence of all?

Yearly inspections

An inspector visited schools once a year to test children on reading, writing and arithmetic. Children had to pass these tests to move up from one class or Standard to another.

Payment by results

It was important for teachers that the pupils did well. If the test results were bad, the school grant was cut and so were teachers' wages. Teachers drilled children to answer exact questions and remember everything they learned off by heart.

Certificates and books

Children who passed the tests were rewarded with certificates and book prizes. Some schools gave children a half day's holiday for good results.

Rewards and treats

School was not all hard work, especially on Friday afternoons and at the end of term. Children went on outings to the zoo, the country or to a park. Sometimes they had a magic lantern show or extra playtime.

This teacher is giving a book prize to a star pupil.

CENSUS DETECTIVE WORK

The census is a record of all the people in the United Kingdom on a particular day and is taken every ten years. The first census was taken in 1801. Census records can provide much information about people's lives in the past.

Looking at a census record

By looking at information collected under the different headings, you can find out where people were living on a particular date, their age, whether they were married, their job, and where they were born.

The table below shows information for two streets in Lavenham, a large village in Suffolk. It is taken from the 1901 census, taken two months after Queen Victoria's death.

Parish of Lavenham			Ecclesiastical Parish of Lavenham		Rural District of Cosford		Parliamentary Borough of Sudbury		Town or Village or Hamlet of Lavenham		
Number on census	Road/street or name of house	Houses inhabited	Houses uninhabited	Name and surname of each person	Relation to head of family	Married or not	Age of Males	Age of Females	Profession or Occupation	Employer, worker or own account	If working at home	Where born	If 1.deaf-and-blind 2.blind 3.imbecile or idiot 4.lunatic
147	45 Prentice St	1		John M Baker	Head	M	39		Miller & Grain Merchant	Employer	At home	Suffolk, Lavenham	
				Ada Baker	Wife	M		36				Surrey, Wimbledon	
				Frederick Baker	Brother	S	34		Miller & Grain Merchant	Employer	At home	Suffolk, Lavenham	
				Lionel J Baker	Son		7					" "	
				Arthur E Baker	Son		6					" "	
				Martha A Wells	Servant	S		18	Cook (domestic)			" "	
				Gertrude Poulson	Servant	S		16	Housemaid (domestic)			" "	
				Maurice G Baker	Son		4					" "	
148	46 Prentice St	1		Harriet Smith	Head	S		77	Own means			" "	
149	1 Bolton St	1		Thomas Smith	Head	M	51		Agricultural labourer	Worker		" "	
				Eunice Smith	Wife	M		54				" "	
				Herbert Smith	Son	S	31		Horsehair sorter	Worker		" "	
				Harry Smith	Son	S	20		Cocomat maker	Worker		" "	
				Arthur J Smith	Son	S	17		Agricultural labourer	Worker		" "	
				Robert S Smith	Son	S	15		Apprentice saddler	Worker		" "	

Focus on the Baker family

Look at the information about the people living at 45 Prentice Street – the Baker family and their servants. Find the entries for three brothers, Lionel, Arthur and Maurice. They are shown in the photo (bottom), wearing identical straw hats.

1 How old were the Baker boys in 1901? The older boys would have gone to school – either the Board School in Lavenham or a Dame school.
2 What job did their father do?
3 How old were their servants, Martha and Gertrude, and how are their jobs described?
4 Look at the 'WHERE BORN' column to see whether people moved house much.
5 Look at the 'Relation to Head of Family' column to see how everybody was connected to the head of the family, Mr John Baker.

Focus on the Smith family

Look at the entry for 1 Bolton Street, where the Smith family lived with their four sons.

1 What ages were the sons?
2 What jobs were they doing?
3 The father and one of the sons were agricultural labourers. Farming employed a lot more people at this time as many jobs were done by hand.
4 Find the entry for Robert. He was only 15 but he was already an apprentice, learning to make saddles and harnesses for horses. Horses pulled farm machinery, carts and wagons, and people rode about on them.
5 Which son worked as a horsehair sorter? Lavenham had a small factory where horsehair (from the mane and tail of the horse) was woven into a tough fabric for covering furniture.
6 Which son was working as a cocomat worker? Another small factory wove coconut fibres into rugs and mats.
7 Can you tell which family were better off – the Bakers or the Smiths?

Now that you've looked at this census return, find out about children and families who lived close to your school during the Victorian period, or investigate your own family history.

Three of the Baker brothers are shown in the front row of this family photo.

TIMELINE

1830s

1837 Queen Victoria came to the throne.

1840s

1840 Rowland Hill invented the Penny Post.

1842 Edwin Chadwick wrote a report about sanitary conditions of working people.

1842 The Mines Act banned boys under the age of ten, and all girls and women, from working in coal mines.

1843 The first Christmas card was sent.

1844 A law was passed saying that factory machinery had to be guarded.

1844 The Ragged Schools Union was set up.

1844 A law was passed saying children in factories had to have three hours of schooling per day.

1850s

1857 The Industrial Schools Act allowed schools to be set up for neglected and homeless children who might turn to crime.

1860s

1861 Prince Albert died of typhoid. Queen Victoria began a long period of deep mourning for her husband.

1862 Headteachers were required to keep log books of details about attendance, illness, visitors, exams and teachers.

1865 An underground sewage system was laid down in London.

1867 The Workshop Act banned children under the age of eight from working in any factory or workshop.

1867 A Factory Act forbade children, young people and women from working on Sundays.

1880s

1880 Schooling for children between the ages of five and ten was made compulsory.

1881 The first electric street lights appeared.

1882/83 Married women now have the right to own their own house.

1885 The 'safety' bicycle, with equal-sized wheels and a chain, was invented.

1886 A Shop Hours Act limited working hours of people under 18 to 74 hours a week.

1887 Queen Victoria's Golden Jubilee.

1887 Queen Victoria medals for perfect attendance were introduced.

1887 The gramophone was invented.

1888 The Football League was founded by twelve clubs.

1891 Basketball was invented.

1891 A Factory Act raised the minimum workin age to eleven.

1891 Schooling was made free.

1840s

1846 Prince Albert made the German custom of decorating a Christmas tree fashionable in England.

1847 The Ten Hours Act reduced the working day in mills for children to ten hours a day.

1847 The first public park opened in Birkenhead, Merseyside. Many other town and city parks followed.

1848 Local boards of health were set up to improve drinking water and sewage systems in towns and cities.

1850s

1850 The Public Libraries Act enabled towns to build free public libraries.

1851 Almost two million children went to Sunday School, according to the 1851 census.

1853 Vaccination against smallpox became compulsory for children.

1854–1856 Britain and France fought the Crimean War against Russia.

1870s

1870 Board Schools were set up for children under the age of ten.

1871 Bank Holidays started.

1871 The Rugby Football Union was formed to set rules for rugby football.

1872 Girls were banned from working in brickyards.

1872 The First FA Cup Final was played.

1874 A Factory Act raised the minimum working age to nine.

1875 Town councils had to start rubbish collections.

1875 Young boys were banned from working as chimney sweeps.

1875 A law allowed slums to be knocked down and replaced with new homes for the poor.

1877 The First Wimbledon tennis championship was held.

1890s

1893 The school leaving age was raised to eleven.

1894 Moving pictures were invented by the Lumière Brothers.

1894 The Prevention of Cruelty to Children Act banned children under eleven from performing or selling things in the street.

1895 The wireless (radio) was invented by Guglielmo Marconi.

1895 The first car factory opened in Birmingham.

1897 Queen Victoria's Diamond Jubilee.

1900s

1899 The school leaving age was raised to twelve.

1899 A survey of York by Seebohm Rowntree found that a quarter of the city's people were living in poverty.

1901 Queen Victoria died.

GLOSSARY

act a law made by Parliament

apprentice a person learning a skill from someone who is already doing it

census an official count of people living in a country

chamber pot a pottery potty

charity an organisation that raises money for good causes and gives help to people or animals in need

cholera a dangerous, often fatal disease caused by drinking or eating dirty water, milk or food

commissioner a person appointed to do a specific task

compulsory something that must be done

copperplate a style of writing in thin, sloping, looped letters

cottage industry work that people do in their own homes, often using their own tools and equipment

court a group of houses built around a small, paved yard

Crimean War a war fought near the Black Sea by Britain, France and Turkey against Russia, from 1854 to 1856

dictation a passage that teachers read aloud for children to write down

epidemic when many people catch a disease or illness at the same time

grant a sum of money given, often by the government, for a particular purpose

industrial relating to industry and factories

inhale to breathe in

inspector someone whose job it is to visit a place, such as a factory or school, to make sure it is run properly

law a rule made by Parliament that everyone must obey

log book a school diary in which the headteacher filled in details of what happened at school each day

moral relating to character or behaviour considered good or bad

night-soil the contents of privies, carried away at night and sometimes used for fertiliser

orphan a child whose parents are both dead

Parliament the place where elected MPs (Members of Parliament) meet to discuss and make laws for the country

parlour a smart sitting room, usually the front room

proverb a short sentence that gives advice or expresses a truth

public school a boarding school for boys, which parents paid for

Ragged School a free Victorian

school for the very poorest children

range a kitchen stove built into the fireplace

ringworm a skin disease caused by a type of fungus

scavenge to search amongst rubbish for things that can be used or eaten

School Board a group of people who set up and ran Board Schools

scullery a room next to a kitchen for washing up, laundry and cleaning

slide a small, transparent picture put into a magic lantern or projector

starch a powder used to make clean clothes stiff, so they did not crease

suburb an area of housing on the edges of towns and cities

Sunday School a school attached to a church where children learned about Christian beliefs and the Bible

trade a job that needs skill and training

tradesmen shopkeepers or skilled workmen who called at houses

typhoid a disease carried by dirty water

ventilation a way of letting fresh air into a room or building

water-closet a small room used as a lavatory with flushing water

workhouse a place where people could eat and sleep in return for work

WEBSITES

These websites can help you find out more about life in Victorian Britain.

www.bbc.co.uk/schools/primary history/victorian_britain/
This BBC website focuses on life for children during Victorian times, and includes information, videos, photographs and activities.

www.nationalarchives.gov.uk/ education/victorians.htm
The National Archives website has a section devoted to the Victorians.

www.nationalarchives.gov.uk/ victorians/
This National Archives microsite encourages the use of history skills to learn about the Victorians.

www.beamish.org.uk/mining-life/
Investigate what happened to a Victorian miner using this web resource, produced by Beamish Museum.

www.chiddingstone.kent.sch.uk/ homework/victorians.html
Follow this link to a site packed with information about Victorian life.

INDEX